War in the Gulf

THE ARAB/ISRAELI CONFLICT

Written By: Paul J. Deegan

Published by Abdo & Daughters, 6535 Cecilia Circle, Edina, Minnesota 55439.

Library bound edition distributed by Rockbottom Books, Pentagon Tower, P.O. Box 36036, Minneapolis, Minnesota 55435.

Library of Congress Number: 91-073073   ISBN: 1-56239-028-7

Cover: Handpainted Rendition by Margaret Coleman Abdo
Inside Photos by: Globe Photos: 29, 41, 47
                            5, 8, 15, 20, 33, 35 (upper), 38, 43, 44
                            11, 17, 23, 27, 30, 35 (lower)

Edited by: Rosemary Wallner

TABLE OF CONTENTS

GULF VICTORY SPAWNS HOPE FOR PEACE

As American armed forces and their coalition allies claimed a quick and easy victory over Iraq in the Persian Gulf War in February 1991, United States President George Bush called for "a new world order." Among the president's aims were peace between the Arab nations of the Persian Gulf region and the Jewish state of Israel.

This would be a dramatic change in the politics of the Middle East. Saying he saw a "window of opportunity" for an Arab-Israeli peace settlement, President Bush sent Secretary of State James Baker on a series of trips to the Middle East in the spring of 1991. Baker tried to lay the groundwork for negotiations on an Arab-Israeli peace agreement. The president himself made personal appeals to Israel and Syria.

The U.S. Armed Forces and their coalition claimed a quick victory over Iraq.
President and 1st Lady Barbara Bush show their support to the troops before
Operation Desert Storm.

NEW NATIONS CARVED OUT OF GREATER SYRIA

Greater Syria (Sirea) has been settled since about 3,500 B.C. This region covered the land southeast of Turkey and east of the Mediterranean Sea. It included much of today's Israel (iz re uhl), Jordan (Jörd uhn), Syria, and Lebanon (Lèbuh nuhn), as well as parts of what was then Turkey (tuhr ke).

Located on major trade routes, Greater Syria was conquered often through the centuries. The Romans took control a year after moving into Palestine (Pal uh stin, or sten). Some 1,400 years later, the area fell to the Turks and was part of the Ottoman (ät uh muhn) Empire until the end of World War I.

Following the defeat of the Ottoman Empire in World War I, the League of Nations sanctioned the division of Greater Syria as drawn up by Britain (Brit uhn) and France. Britain gained control of Palestine in the southwest and neighboring Transjordan (Tran(t)s Jörd uhn) (later named Jordan). France (Fran(t)s) was given control of Syria and its Mount Lebanon region.

JEWS SEEK PALESTINE

When the British took control of Palestine, they were aware that establishing a Jewish homeland in their biblical homeland was a dream of many Jews.

In 1020 B.C. the Hebrews, also known as Jews, had ruled a kingdom in the region that is today's Israel. The Hebrew religion was Judaism.

The region included the biblical places of Jerusalem (Juh rü s(uh)luhm), Bethlehem (Beth le huhm), Hebron (He bruhn), and Jericho (Jer i ko). After occupying the area in 63 B.C. and naming it Palestine, the Romans forced the Jews from the area. The Jews dispersed throughout the world. Events began taking place in the late 1800s which some 50 years later would make the dream a reality.

In 1882 Jews fleeing persecution in Russia (Ruhsh uh) and Romania (Ro maa ne uh) formed the first major immigration of Jewish settlers to Palestine. These Eastern Europeans took up a new life in the Middle East, a region populated mostly by Arab Moslems, including those already living in Palestine.

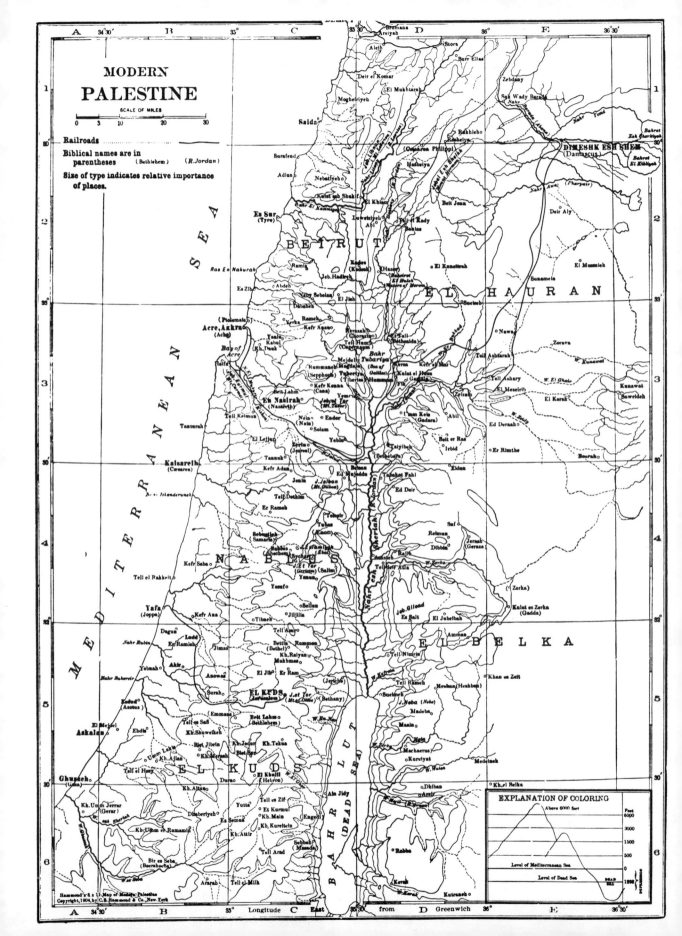

MODERN
PALESTINE

SCALE OF MILES

0   5   10   20   30

Railroads

Biblical names are in
parentheses   (Bethlehem)   (R.Jordan)

Size of type indicates relative importance
of places.

EXPLANATION OF COLORING

Above 6000 feet

Feet
6000
3000
1500
500
Level of Mediterranean Sea
0
Level of Dead Sea
1292

Hammond's 8 x 11 Map of Modern Palestine
Copyright, 1904, by C. S. Hammond & Co., New York.

Longitude   East   from   Greenwich

Middle Eastern Arabs were not happy with the idea of a new Jewish state in their midst. While the Ottoman Empire still held Palestine, Arab leaders in Jerusalem asked the Turks to prohibit Jewish immigration to Palestine. Nevertheless, the movement to set up a Jewish state gained strength in the last years of the 1800s. Theodor Herzl, an Austrian journalist, founded modern Zionism, the movement backing the creation of a Jewish state. Herzl wanted Jews to be able to live freely without fear of persecution.

There was a good-sized Jewish population, some 60,000, living in Palestine by 1916. The overall population of Palestine at the time was some 700,000. At least half of the Jewish population had come from Russia, choosing the hardships of pioneer life in Palestine over persecution in Eastern Europe (Yu[1] uhp).

In an area which has few natural resources, the settlers worked to restore the barren soil. They drained swamps and irrigated deserts. By the early 1920s their settlements had begun to prosper. Zionism brought encouragement and support came from abroad.

BRITAIN SEPARATES PALESTINE

Although they supported the idea of a Jewish "national home" in Palestine, in 1921 Britain divided Palestine. The area east of the Jordan River, some three-fourths of the total land area of Palestine, became an Arab kingdom, the Emirate of Transjordan, today's Jordan.

There were some 300,000 Arabs in Transjordan. Half were nomadic Bedouins; half Palestinian Arabs who lived on the East Bank of the river.

Palestinian Arabs and Zionist Jews both wanted the western area of Palestine, between the Jordan and the Mediterranean Sea. The conflict became more heated as Jewish survivors of World War II flooded into Palestine.

After the war, Britain said it was going to withdraw from the western half of Palestine and extract itself from the problem of who was going to have this land. Britain turned the matter over to the United Nations (U.N.).

Nomadic Bedouin tribesmen living in the desolatae country of Jordan.

On November 29, 1947, the U.N. General Assembly voted to divide western Palestine into two states. One would be for the Jews; the other for the Palestinian Arabs.

The Jews were to get the coastal plain running from Haifa in the north to Tel Aviv, and parts of northern Galilee (Gal uh le) and the Negev Desert in the southern half of the small, narrow region.

The Palestinian state was to include the West Bank of the Jordan River, the Gaza District or Gaza Strip along the Mediterranean Sea coast above the Negev, and the Arab sectors of Galilee. The West Bank included Bethlehem, Hebron, and Jericho.

Neither Jews nor Arabs were to get Jerusalem, revered by both Judaism and Islam as a holy city. It was to become an international enclave under U.N. trusteeship.

The Zionists, led by David Ben-Gurion, accepted the proposal. The Palestinan Arabs and the adjoining Arab nations rejected it, believing that all of Palestine was theirs and that they could force out the Jews.

ISRAEL EXISTS
BUT MUST FIGHT TO STAY

On May 14, 1948, just before the British finished withdrawing, the Zionists declared the creation of the State of Israel. The next day the Arabs launched a war to acquire all of western Palestine. The attackers included the Palestinians and armies from Egypt, Jordan, Iraq (i ra k), Lebanon, Saudi Arabia (Saüd e A ra be uh), and Syria.

The Arabs had miscalculated. During the war, Israel not only held on to all the areas given to them by the United Nations, but it seized some of the area the United Nations had assigned to be a Palestinian state.

When the fighting was over, Israel incorporated the additional territory, gaining some 150,000 resettled Palestinian Arabs. Israel now also occupied the western half of Jerusalem. Jordan controlled the eastern half.

Jordan and Egypt took over the other areas intended for the Palestinians. Jordan annexed the West Bank and Egypt took over the Gaza (Gäz uh) Strip at the southeastern edge of the Mediterranean Sea.

Also, hundreds of thousands of Palestinians fled their homes during the war and became refugees in the areas of Palestine not held by Israel and in neighboring Arab countries.

PEACE BUT NO PEACE

In 1949 Israel held its first elections. The former Zionist leader Chaim Weizman became the nation's first president. David Ben-Gurion, another activist in the establishment of the Jewish state, became prime minister.

Although Israel had signed separate armistice agreements with Egypt, Jordan, Lebanon, and Syria following the 1948 war, the fighting wasn't over.

Israel's Arab neighbors continued to allow Palestinian resistance fighters to raid Israel from their territories. Many of the raids came from the Gaza Strip. In 1956 Israel struck back. Assisted by British and French forces, Israel attacked Gamel Abdel Nasser's Egypt and occupied most of the Sinai Peninsula (Si ni Puh nin(t) s(uh) luh). Israel eventually withdrew from the Sinai when the United Nations set up a multinational peace force there and in the Gaza Strip.

Because of all the rioting in the Gaza Strip, Israel handed over control of the area to a U.N. Emergency force.

FRANCE FREES SYRIA

Immediately north and northwest of what was once Palestine, the area of Greater Syria given to France was now two nations — Syria and Lebanon.

Syria was one of the Arab nations with which Israel had been fighting. In Lebanon, events were taking place which also would bring that nation into conflict with Israel.

Syria gained its independence from France in 1946. Control of the government changed hands several times after the first of many military revolts took place in 1949. In 1958 Syria joined Egypt in forming the United Arab Republic. Syria withdrew from the relationship and resumed its independence on September 29, 1961.

The Baath Party, an Arab socialist political organization, gained power in Syria in the early 1960s. A Baathist leader and air force general, Hafez al Assad, became president of Syria in 1971.

Hafez al Assad, President of Syria.

MORE WAR

In 1967 Syria, Egypt (e juhpt), and Jordan began building up their forces along the Israeli border. They blockaded Israel's ships. In June 1967 Israel launched a surprise attack against the three Arab nations. Israel said they struck because they were about to be attacked. The fighting lasted only six days, thus the conflict is known as the Six-Day War. A United Nations cease-fire ended the fighting.

During the brief war, the Israeli army occupied much more territory. They retook the Sinai Peninsula, the 13-mile wide desert which had gone back to Egypt; took control of the Gaza Strip from Egypt; and held Jordan's West Bank, including East Jerusalem, and Syria's Golan Heights. The Gaza Strip and the West Bank were home to one million Palestinians.

The following November the United Nations Security Council passed the famous Resolution 242 dealing with the results of the Six-Day War. This resolution was still the basis for peace proposals in the area 24 years later.

On October 6, 1973, which was Yom Kippur, the most sacred Jewish holy day, Syrian and Egyptian troops made a surprise attack on Israeli forces occupying the Sinai Peninsula and the Golan Heights. After initial Egyptian and Syrian advances, Israeli troops pushed them back.

This was a major conflict in which Israel suffered heavy losses in both soldiers and equipment. The United States supplied Israel with arms during this war and helped negotiate a cease-fire.

WARS ENLARGE ISRAEL

So in war after war, the Arab nations surrounding Israel tried, unsuccessfully, to destroy it. Instead Israel expanded the areas of Palestine which it controlled by taking territories from the Arab states.

Most of the West Bank, which Israel refers to as Judea (Jü de uh) and Samaria (Suh mer e uh); the Gaza Strip; and southern Lebanon are referred to as the occupied territories. East Jersualem on the West Bank and the Golan Heights have been annexed by Israel.

The battles continue throughout all of Israel.

East Jerusalem, was quickly annexed by Israel. It includes Jerusalem's Old City, sacred ground to Jews, Moslems, and Christians. Israel reasserted that the reunified Jerusalem, which has had a Palestinian majority since the 1948 Arab-Israeli war, was the capital of the Jewish state.

The Golan Heights, taken from Syria in the Six-Day War was annexed in 1981. It is 500 square miles of mostly empty, barren plateau, brown from lack of rain for most of the year. So why did Israel annex it?

The reason is that all of Israel's upper Galilee area can be fired upon from the Golan Heights. Many Israelis died during decades of shellings by Syrian gunners on the Heights. That won't be repeated while Israel controls the region.

The Sinai Peninsula, also taken by Israel in the Six-Day War was returned to Egypt. President Anwar Sadat of Egypt went to Jerusalem in 1977 where he spoke to the Israeli parliament. Sadat offered full peace in exchange for a total Israeli withdrawal from the Sinai. Israel returned the Sinai to Egypt as part of a 1979 peace treaty signed by the two nations in Washington, D.C. Egypt is the only Arab nation which has made peace with Israel.

LEBANON FRACTURES

Meanwhile, north of Israel and west of Syria, events were taking place in Lebanon which would lead in the late 1970s to an entanglement of the Arab-Jewish conflict and a Lebanese civil war.

People had been living in what is now Lebanon since the days of prehistory. In the fourth century, Christianity was introduced to the region. In the early 600s, Moslems from the Arabian Peninsula occupied the region. From 1516 until the end of World War I, the region was under the control of the Ottoman Empire.

Throughout the centuries, a Christian community remained intact in the mountains of north central Lebanon, east of Beirut (Ba ͑rüt), today Lebanon's capital and major city. The Christians on Mount Lebanon were Maronites, an Eastern church founded in Syria some 1,600 years ago which was allied with Roman Catholicism. The Maronites maintained a relationship with France since French knights established kingdoms in the area during the Crusades in the 1100s. The Crusaders were driven out of Lebanon by an Egyptian dynasty about 1300.

VIEW OF ANCIENT BEIRUT, LEBANON.

People have been living in what is now Lebanon since the times of prehistory.

LEBANON'S POLITICS BASED UPON RELIGION

After World War I, the Maronites persuaded France to establish a Lebanese state. The Maronites wanted the new state to include Moslem regions — the coastal cities and the valleys of south Lebanon — in order to achieve greater economic stability.

The coastal cities were basically Arab Sunni Moslem communities. The valleys were Arab Shiite Moslem regions. Sharing the rugged mountains with the Maronites were the Druse, a splinter sect of Islam. Moslems and Christians would each have about half the population of the proposed "Greater Lebanon."

No one, however, had asked the Arab Moslems if they wanted to be part of a new Lebanon. Many were unhappy about the prospect. The Moslems wanted to become part of Arab Moslem's Syria.

France ignored the Moslems' concerns and in 1920 decreed the formation of a state of Greater Lebanon, embracing the areas proposed by the Maronites. It took 23 more years to make it official, but the modern republic of Lebanon includes the cities of Beirut, Tripoli, Sidon, and Tyre on the coast, the Mount Lebanon region, and the Akkar and the Bekaa Valley in the south.

It was 1943 before Moslem leaders in Lebanon reached agreement with the Christians. The Maronites agreed to sever their bond with France and OK'd the idea that Lebanon would be called an Arab nation. The Moslems in turn withdrew their demand for a union with Syria. The unwritten agreement was called the National Pact.

The pact said that Lebanon's president would always be a Maronite and that Christians would have a majority of the seats in parliament. The foreign minister would always be a Sunni Moslem and the speaker of the parliament always a Shiite.

On December 27, 1943, an agreement between France and the independent republic of Lebanon transferred most of the powers of government to Lebanon. The new nation had the most Christians of any Arab nation and retained a close relationship with Western nations.

Lebanon was peaceful under the divided political arrangement until the 1970s with one exception. In 1958 some Lebanese, most of them Moslems, objected to planned political and military alliances with the West and rebelled against the government. The United States sent some 15,000 Marines to Lebanon in July 1958 when asked to do so by the Lebanese government. After peace was restored, the Marines left in October.

MOSLEMS OUTNUMBER CHRISTIANS, SIDE WITH PLO

By the 1970s, however, the Lebanese Moslem and Druse communities had grown much larger, numbering almost two-thirds of the population. There were now about twice as many Moslems as Christians. Also, the Shiites had become the nation's largest group, bypassing both the Sunnis and the Christians in numbers.

The Moslems wanted more power in the nation's government. However, the Maronites were not interested in changing the terms of the 1943 arrangement. The Christians formed private armies to support their position. The two best known were the Phalangist militia and the Tigers militia. The Moslems and Druse also formed private armies to help them enforce their demands.

In 1964, the leaders of the Arab nations, acting through the Arab League, had organized the Palestinian resistance groups as the Palestinian Liberation Organization (PLO).

After the Arab nations disastrous defeat in the Six-Day War, independent Palestinian guerrilla groups, upset by the Arab nations inability to remove the Jewish nation, took control of the PLO. In 1969 they elected a guerrilla named Yasir Arafat to head them.

Yasir Arafat (right) holding onto his Russian made machine gun.

A year later, however, the PLO was defeated by the Jordanian army in a civil war over control of Jordan. Driven out of Jordan, Arafat and the PLO still had a stronghold in Lebanon.

In 1974, the PLO was declared to be the "sole and legitimate representative of the Palestinian people." This declaration was made at an Arab summit meeting in Rabat, Morocco, in 1974.

CONFLICTS INTERTWINED

Lebanese Moslems and Druse befriended the PLO, most of whom also were Moslems. Not only did they support the PLO's objectives, the Lebanese believed the PLO could help them in their attempt to gain additional power from the Maronite Christians. The PLO basically became the Moslem's largest private militia.

The PLO raids against Israel resulted in Israeli military counterattacks on PLO forces in Lebanon. This in turn caused the Lebanese Christians to urge the government to use the Lebanese army to destroy the PLO in Lebanon.

Fighting breaks out in the occupied territory between PLO youths and Israeli security forces.

29

A more peaceful Beirut, Lebanon.

SYRIANS ENTER LEBANON

In the spring of 1976, under an Arab League peacekeeping mandate, Syria sent thousands of soldiers into Lebanon to try to end the fighting. The Syrians gained control over the rest of Lebanon including the area around the port city of Tripoli in the north and the Bekka Valley in the west.

Life was more peaceful in Beirut, beginning in 1976, after the worst fighting ended. However, there were now numerous private armies in the country, "each," according to Friedman, "amply funded by one or another Arab regime." These private militias continued to fight among themselves. There were also battles between the Christian forces and the Syrian troops. A United Nations peacekeeping force sent to Lebanon in 1978 could not end the armed clashes.

ISRAELIS INVADE LEBANON

In June 1982 Israel invaded Lebanon. The Israelis drove the PLO from southern Lebanon and successfully attacked western Beirut. At the demand of the Israelis, the PLO left Beirut in the late summer of 1982.

The Christians wanted to restore peace in Lebanon, but they also wanted to eliminate the PLO as an ally of the Moslems. The Moslems, of course, opposed turning the Lebanese army against the PLO.

Caught between the two historic rivals, the Lebanese government did nothing. So the Christian private armies moved against the PLO. As time went by, Christians in the Lebanese army joined the cause. Moslem soldiers did likewise. There were battles in the streets of Beirut.

By 1975 the conflict had become a major civil war. Tens of thousands were killed and there was heavy damage to property. Neither side could establish power. When the government collapsed, Lebanon became informally divided. The south of Lebanon and west Beirut, which was mostly Moslem and where most government institutions and foreign embassies were located, were controlled by the PLO and the Moslem militias.

East Beirut, the Christian area of the city, and the Christian areas on Mount Lebanon were controlled by the Christian private armies.

Israeli soldiers invade Beirut, Lebanon.

Backed by Israel, the Christian Phalangists had convinced the Lebanese parliament to elect the militia's leader, Bashir Gemayel, president of the country. Bashir had struck a deal with the Israeli government to mount a joint effort to drive the PLO and the Syrians out of Lebanon. However, 22 days after his election, Bashir was assassinated by a Syrian intelligence agent.

A few days later, Phalangist militiamen massacred hundreds of unarmed Palestinian civilians in two refugee camps in West Beirut while the camps were surrounded by Israeli forces.

Bashir's older brother, Amin, became president and within a few months the Lebanese Moslems had allied themselves with the Syrians and the Lebanese civil war was once again at full tilt. Giving up on their plan to impose controls on Lebanon, Israel on its own began to withdraw its forces from Lebanon in September 1983.

When Israel's army had captured Beirut, U.S. Marines had come to Beirut as part of a multinational peacekeeping force. These troops were still in Lebanon in the fall of 1983. On October 23, a suicide terrorist drove a truck full of explosives into Marine headquarters in Beirut. The explosion killed 241 U.S. troops.

Beshir Gemayel,
former president
of Lebanon.

PLO Leader Yasir Arafat and President Sadat of Egypt.

35

In February 1984, Lebanese Moslem forces revolted against the Lebanese army and took control of part of Beirut from President Amin's government. When this happened, the Lebanese government once again fell apart. The United States and the other Western nations withdrew their peacekeeping force. The following year, Israel completed the withdrawal of all of its troops from most of Lebanon. The Israelis kept a security zone along the Lebanon-Israel border.

After the Israelis drove the PLO from Beirut in 1982, Arafat eventually found a haven in North Africa, far from the Palestinians' home. Half of all Palestinians were now living under Israeli occupation.

In early December 1987 clashes between Israelis and Palestinians in the Gaza Strip erupted into a full scale uprising by the 1.7 million Palestinians in Gaza and the West Bank. What was known in Arabic as the *intifada* was underway. By June 1991 the revolt against Israeli rule had lasted for 42 months.

LEBANON TODAY

"Lebanon was once known as the Switzerland of the Middle East," according to Middle East expert Thomas Friedman. It was "a land of mountains, money, and many cultures, all of which somehow miraculously managed to live together in harmony. At least that was the picture-postcard view." Lebanon also is the only Middle Eastern country south of Turkey which has sufficient ground water to meet its needs.

By late 1990 it was a fractured, battered, war-torn, weary country. Some 150,000 Lebanese had been killed in the civil war which had gone on for almost 16 years. The old downtown area of Beirut, once the heart of the city, was devastated. Amidst the collapsed buildings, wild grass grew six-feet high on abandoned roads. Mountains of garbage were commonplace in the city, government services having long ago collapsed.

However, in December 1990 there was hope among the 3.5 million Lebanese that the carnage might have come to a halt. A 250-square-mile zone had been created in Beirut and the surrounding areas which were free of private armies. Government services were beginning to be restored.

A civilian carrying a wounded child runs among debris after a booby trapped car exploded in a street in Beirut.

The armies had withdrawn from Beirut under an agreement worked out the previous year. The Arab nations had gotten Lebanese, Christian and Moslem legislators together in Saudi Arabia. An agreement on ending the civil war was hammered out, calling for the private armies to be disbanded in the spring of 1991.

At the 1990 meeting, the Christians and Moslems also agreed to rearrange the balance of political power. The 1943 pact giving Christians a majority in parliament was changed so that power was equally divided between Christians and Moslems. Also, President Elias Hrawi's cabinet now has 15 members from each of the two religious groups. Hrawi became president after Rene Muaward was assassinated on November 22, 1989, making Muaward the second Lebanese president to meet such a fate a few days after being elected.

When the private armies left the Beirut region, they reassembled in other parts of the country. The Christian militias were north and northeast of Beirut. The Moslem militias were in eastern and southern Lebanon. All still were heavily armed.

As 1991 began, the Beirut area was the only part of Lebanon the government really controlled. There were 6,000 Lebanese army troops there along with 3,000 policemen supported by the Syrian army, the main powerbroker in Lebanon. The Syrians had been in Lebanon since 1976 and in the spring of 1991, 40,000 Syrian troops controlled an estimated 70 percent of the country.

The Syrians "provide Hrawi's military muscle and remain the final arbiter," a reporter said in Beirut. To that end, Lebanon and Syria signed a cooperation treaty on June 3, 1991. Hrawi was depending on the Syrian presence to bring stability to Lebanon. Maybe the violence was over. Earlier, in April, the largest Christian militia, the Lebanese Forces, had agreed to turn over their heavy weapons to the army under the Arab League peace plan. The largest Moslem militia began handing over its large weapons to the Syrians.

The other major Moslem private army, the Syria-leaning Shiite Amal, had already given up most of its heavy weapons. "The (civil) war has ceased to be a tool for political change," said one Lebanese businesswoman.

However, there were still plenty of people with arms in Lebanon in addition to the Lebanese army and the Syrian soldiers. The PLO had 6,000 men in southern Lebanon. Also in the south, there were 2,500 members of the South Lebanon Army, an Israeli-supported militia, along a border strip occupied by 1,000 Israeli soldiers. There also were 6,000 Iranian Revolutionary Guards in eastern Lebanon.

The PLO had 6,000 men fighting in southern Lebanon; above is a 13-year-old Palestinian boy displaying his Russian-made rifle.

SYRIA TODAY

The presidency is the most powerful office under the 1973 constitution of The Syrian Arab Republic. Assad remains Syria's leader, strictly controlling the country of over 11 million who live over 71,500 square miles.

Damascus, the capital of Syria, is one of the world's most famous cities. Over one million people live there today.

Eighty-seven percent of the Syrian people are Moslems, most of them Sunni. The rest of the population is mostly Orthodox Christian.

In February 1982, Assad's government massacred thousands of its own citizens. Some 20,000 Moslems were killed after they had started a rebellion from the town of Hama, Syria's fourth-largest city.

Friedman says Assad could kill his own citizens "because on some level Assad did not see these Sunni Moslem(s) . . . as part of his nation or as fellow citizens. He saw then as members of an alien tribe — strangers in the desert . . ."

Syria did participate in the U.S.-led coalition against Iraq, even though prior to this conflict Assad had been considered an enemy of the United States. Israeli leaders point out that Syria got $3 billion from the United States for taking part in the coalition.

*Syrian President
Hafez al Assad*

ISRAEL TODAY

The huge movement of Soviet immigrants to
Israel — 250,000 from late 1989 until June 1991 —
provides another challenge for the government of
Israeli Prime Minister Yitzhak Shamir. Chaim
Herzog is president of the democratic republic.
There are almost 6 million people living in Israel
and in the West Bank. Israel had only a little over
800,000 at its birth in 1948. Some four million of
today's population are Jews. Over half a million
are Arabs.

*Israeli Prime Minister
Yitzhak Shamir*

Israel's 8,000 square miles occupy about one quarter of the territory mandated to Britain as Palestine some 70 years ago. The occupied territories measure another 4,000 square miles. Although Israel is a narrow strip of land, 360 miles long and 70 miles at its widest point, it embraces seashores, mountains, valleys, and deserts.

Israel did not participate in the Persian Gulf War even after Iraq fired Scud missiles into Israel, trying to draw the Israelis into the conflict. The United States did not want Israel to fight Iraq because this would have given the Arab world a reason to support Iraq.

PEACE OBSTACLES LOOM

Will Israel survive? This is a question that after more than 40 years still hasn't been answered. Also, the Palestinians, after turning down the 1948 U.N. proposal, still have no territory they can call their own.

With the defeat of Iraq in the Gulf War, Israel today views Syria as their most dangerous foe. No other Arab nation poses a military threat to Israel. When Syria signed the treaty with Lebanon in June 1991, Israel feared the agreement would lead to increased attacks by Palestinian guerillas and Moslem militia based in southern Lebanon. For three days in June, Israeli warplanes attacked these bases.

Earlier, as part of the effort led by President Bush to get peace talks started, Secretary of State Baker, reputedly held in high regard by the Arab nations, made four trips to the Middle East. Syria and Israel were key stops. The cooperation of Syria's Assad, analysts said, was a key to any successful peace conference. And there could be no talks unless Israel participated.

Israeli Jews, however, were angrier than ever at the Palestinians because most Palestinians had supported Iraq in the Gulf War. Despite United States requests to ease its control of the

Palestinians, the Israelis accelerated their anti-Palestinian measures, speeding up the building of houses for Jews on the West Bank among other things. Baker said in May 1991 that Israel's continuing settlement of the West Bank was the biggest obstacle he was facing in trying to initiate peace talks.

The question of who would represent the Palestinian people if any peace talks came about also was unresolved. Israel did not intend to deal with the PLO, which demands an independent Palestinian state. Prime Minister Shamir also refused to consider Palestinians from Jerusalem as representatives of the Palestinian Arabs. Shamir did not want to give any sign that Israel would consider negotiating the return of part of that city, which Israelis consider their capital.

Saudi Arabia had already said they would not participate in any Mideast peace conference. And Baker had not found any real interest in Damascus toward moving peace talks ahead. As the summer of 1991 began, any chance for movement toward a lasting solution to the longstanding Arab-Israeli conflict seemed remote.

Palestinian women demonstrate for the return of their land, now occupied by the Israeli's.

GLOSSARY

ALLIANCE(S): A formal agreement between nations.

ANNEX(ED): Bring a territory into a nation.

ARBITER: One who has the power to decide.

ARMISTICE: A temporary halt to fighting.

ASSASSINATED: Murdered.

BLOCKADE(D): Close off a harbor.

CONSTITUTION: A system of laws.

DEMOCRATIC: A system of government by the people directly or through elected representatives.

DYNASTY: A succession of rulers from the same family.

ENCLAVE: An area within a larger unit.

GUERILLA: Member of an irregular fighting force.

IMMIGRATION: Movement to another country.

ISLAM: A religion based upon the teachings of the prophet Mohammed.

NOMAD(IC): People who have no permanent home and move from place to place.

PARLIAMENT: A national body of elected representatives.

REPUBLIC: A system of government where the head of state is not a king and is usually a president.

SECT: A group forming a unit within a larger group on the basis of a difference in belief.

SOCIALIST: Favoring a system in which the producers have both political power and the control of producing goods.

SPLINTER: A group which had broken away from another group.

TRUSTEESHIP: Administer a territory or region under the direction of a worldwide organization.

UNDERCLASS: The lowest group in a society.

956
DEE

Deegan, Paul J

The Arab/Israeli
conflict

DATE DUE   11815